Wildflower. Stone.

Wildflower. Stone.

poems

Marian Haddad

Pecan Grove Press San Antonio, Texas

Library of Congress Cataloging-in-Publication Data

Haddad, Marian.
Wildflower. Stone. : poems / by Marian Haddad.
p. cm.
ISBN 978-1-931247-85-6 (alk. paper)
I. Title.
PS3608.A265W56 2011
811'.6--dc22
2010032780

Pecan Grove Press
Box AL
1 Camino Santa Maria
San Antonio, TX 78228

Acknowledgments and Gratitude

Grateful acknowledgment is made to the editors and publishers of these anthologies in which these poems first appeared (some as previous versions):

"Dark Sky: Outside My Coast Boulevard Apartment, La Jolla, California" appeared in *Stories from Where We Live: The California Coast,* edited by Sara St. Antoine, Milkweed Editions, 2001

"Wildflower. Stone." first appeared as an essay comprising a number of poems around which narrative was built in *Pride of Place: A Contemporary Anthology of Texas Nature Writing,* edited by David Taylor, UNT Press, 2006

"Only the Sky Can Heal the Frightened Eye" appeared in *Between Heaven and Texas,* photographs by Wyman Meinzer, poems selected by Naomi Shihab Nye, introduction by Sarah Bird, University of Texas Press, 2006

"Ozona" appeared in *A Student's Treasury of Texas Poetry,* edited by Billy Bob Hill, TCU Press, 2007

"Gruene, Texas: At the River," "I am walking back," "Watching the World from a Corner Table," "In a San Diego Courtyard," "Accidental Resting," "Time," and "Driving from El Paso to San Antonio" appeared in *In these Latitudes: Ten Contemporary Poets,* edited by Robert Bonazzi, Wings Press, 2009 (particular thanks to the generous space Robert Bonazzi afforded each featured poet).

Many thanks to the following journals, online journals/websites, and newspapers/periodicals for including the following poems:

"A Psalm for a Mother," *Pecan Grove Review*; "My father's garden," *Radius of Arab American Writers (RAWI) Online*; "Upon Driving: Santa Teresa, New Mexico (five miles from El Paso)" and "Statue of the Sleeping," *San Antonio Express News*; and "Looking Outside My Airplane Window: San Diego, California" and "Dark Sky," *San Diego Writers' Monthly.*

"Dark Sky," "Creeping," and "On a Day Where I Must Stay in" appear in *Saturn Falling Down,* a limited-edition, numbered and signed chapbook compiled at the request of Texas Public Radio in correlation with their Hands-On Poetry Workshops, 2003.

First thanks go to Glover Davis who instilled in me the sheer necessity of musical cadence in all verse, formal or free, and who still directs the orchestra in my head as I write. Endless gratitude to H. Palmer Hall for the astonishing amount of work he does for the love of poetry; and great thanks to him for giving the poets he publishes, oftentimes, a platform for the first time, while publishing many who have had a number of books previously published. I am proud to have had two collections of my poetry represented by his press. To dear Luis Cortez at Pecan Grove who has been and continues to be a joy and a blessing. Wild thanks to Naomi Shihab Nye whose work spoke to me the first day I opened a book of her poems; gratitude to her for her light, energy and generosity. For Mother and Father, for their being my first teachers of poetry, language and music; for teaching me a deep love for the land and a great gratitude for the blessings of the natural world steeped in a deep-rooted love for God. For Elroy Bode, who is, to me, both Whitmanian and Steinbeckian, who speaks to this heart as a poet/priest through his prose. For the many family members, friends, poets, instructors and colleagues across the country and outside it, who've heard the poems through and helped me to hear. For my students of all ages and backgrounds who have given me joy and who continue to teach me, as well, through their distinct voices and work. For Ramin Samandari, who allowed his elegant and powerful photographic images to grace this cover. For the desert terrain, my second mother—that birthed and raised me; and for the sea and rivers and every body of water that causes me to worship the reflective sky and its Maker. And lastly, but most definitely not least, for the enlightened heart of Michael Joseph Jackson, whose love and gratitude for "the infinity of forms" and "the Creator" has been and will continue to be an inspiration to this spirit—who through his work and words, further instills in me the necessity and reality of grace and gratitude.

For earth and sea and sky
Water, river, earth

For constellations
Perpetual rebirth

For galaxies and air
The four directions of flight

And for the Maker of them
And for the Science of Light

It's hard to feel regret
where the air's so big
all the days we haven't lived yet
breathe in and out
their grand extravagance ...

—**Naomi Shihab Nye**

Contents

I. Anything that Grows by the Sea Has Secrets

II. Wildflower. Stone.

III. Yellow Buds of the Desert; Birds of Paradise

Foreword

Wildflower. Stone. is Marian Haddad's lyrical/narrative paean to the lands that have shaped her life and poetry: from El Paso to San Antonio, San Antonio to the wild beauty of the Texas Gulf Coast, to her adopted city of San Diego and the highways that connect them. Haddad, in poetry that is a contemporary praisesong to life writes of the interconnectedness of all things—literally and figuratively.

Wildflower. Stone. reminds us that the common can become uncommon, that highways are more than just a physical means of transportation, that deserts, oceans, mountains are both formations and transformations.

Wildflower. Stone. continues the development of natural themes Haddad has been celebrating since the publication of her first chapbook, Saturn Falling Down, and her first full length book, Somewhere Between Mexico and a River Called Home, also from Pecan Grove Press.

Wildflower. Stone. is, ultimately, a celebration of God and of God-in-Nature. A modern continuation of the work of such writers as Henry David Thoreau and John Muir, this is a transcendent song celebrating the world in which we all live.

—H. Palmer Hall
San Antonio, Texas 2010

I.

Anything that Grows by the Sea Has Secrets

We have lingered in the chambers of the sea ...

And the pool was filled with water out of sunlight ...

So the darkness shall be the light, and the stillness the dancing.
Whisper of running streams ...

—T. S. Eliot

Her Body Is a Guitar

for Hal Marcus—after Wallace Stevens

Through this blue guitar
the unconscious river sings.
Empty socket of an eye
through which this river springs.

Body of woman
entwined about helm and prow
of song and strings, rivulets
of cadences between brows.

Body of wood and flesh
dressed in blues and violets
colors of sky and sound
colors of woman wound

about hips of harmonies
wide as water.

River

The way it would feel to catch
this roll of water—to slide
down   this river's narrow mouth.

Looking Outside My Airplane Window: San Diego, California

Burgeoning backdrop of tropical flowers,
burgeoning backdrop of bougainvillea,
of water-hyacinth and sea-salt, this mist
that covers the southernmost cliffs
of this southernmost city.
City of water and cliffs—
of Adam's husks in the garden.

This is the garden of field and flowers,
this body of water,
this body in motion.

Ocean mist, ocean breeze,
this land by the sea.
Here the mermaids whisper
their secrets, as they rise
to sea's surface,
during the hours of our sleep.

On a Day Where I Must Stay in

Don't go out to the sea, Mother says.
You are weak, and the water will find you
easy to take in. There are many living things
by the sea, and you are weak.

So, instead, I sit here in the sun.
It comes down on my head like the burning
shadow of light. It makes things
invisible, I cannot see the way I used to.
And who says something is lost in this light?
Sun nourishes skin, blood, beating
heart, and I am alive again
in its quiet light.

Don't go out to the sea, Mother says,
but all I can see through the mind's pale eye
are the waves, the smell of them,
the sound of their crashing
against sea stones
and the birds singing
their high-pitched caw.

Gruene, Texas
at the River

I came here because
I know this place—because
I have been here before,
and I know where the river
ends—I sit by the part
where it foams
white above rocks—three
stumps reach far down into this
river—and there, across
from me, one seems to be
growing right out of cliff,
right out of rock. It leans—
graceful sway of trunk—it has
somehow found its leaning
comfortable, a sideways growing—
if something stays bent
long enough—it assumes its place
gracefully—learns to live
with that

I am walking back

to the bubbling center
of this river—
I cannot drop my pen—
I walk while I write.
This is how I pray.

Seaflowers

La Jolla, California

In the morning   in the mist   I take the hour
and walk a steady stride by the side of the sea.

The tide high, the surf up   and the sound
of water breaking against low cliffs.

Purple flowers stand straight up, dispersed
between brush. Colors   are clearer—in this light;

green grows deeper against bluegrey.   I take
a different turn today   go down the walk

of the curved wall that juts   out into
the ocean; and I am closer to the water here.

I stand above it   a wave breaks hard
against this wall, casting its live foam up

and on me. The air fresh   sea mist
on my skin   and the sea birds flying

some this way   some that—   I come back
up the walk—   there, a white bird perched

atop a kiosk's brown eaves, the long beak
pointed downward   the bird scratches steady

the skin by its beak; perhaps bird lice
or a tic   a flea   is the cause of this

metronomic movement of the one birdfoot raised up
as the other balances the body   like a dancer;

and the birdfoot scratches   back and forth
and back   and forth—   and I turn the curved

path; a woman carrying a seaflower   like a wand
passes me—   I call it seaflower.   I do not know

the name of its birth; I wonder how many seaflowers
she has picked from the land by other seas.

Something must have made her stop to stoop,
break the base from its root   carry it with her

its own bouquet.   Perhaps magic—is what she seeks.
I go up that dirt path   up against the cliff,

the smell of fish   and seaweed   and protein of sea.
And there I look upon a bush of orange seaflowers,

one seems missing from its place.   The one
the woman took.   It must be seeping secrets

into her skin.   Anything that grows by the sea
has secrets   things close to the earth   and

the water—   How many flowers must she carry?
I jog a quick pace   down the creaking stairs,

walk across a plank of wooden boards,
swirl and sound of water—underneath my feet;

I lean a minute against white beams that fence
this bridge; rusted nails hold this place

together, the earth scooped underneath,
where water nestles and speaks to trees,

a large palm   standing   like a tower
in this circular space, summed up between rocks

that water smoothed.   Up again I go, treading
this familiar hill, this thin road between houses

that overlook the sea. I am closer to the fog here,
and the air, thick with the scent   of anise

or so it seems; and so I look to see which bushes bear
this sweet scent.   It must be these.   Small yellow

flowers; fennel flowers.   I wonder   if I put one
in my mouth   if it would taste   of this day;

if I would close my eyes   I might break   into flight
and as I open   them—   my wing would graze

the water   as I glide low over it—a troop of birds
behind me—   and I would rise back up   and swoop

back down   and up again   and down
some dance we would wing over the sea;   and we

would fly—   *up*   and *up*   and *up*
—the flavor of anise   still strong   in our mouths.

The Japanese Garden

Water trickling
over river rocks
the color of earth—

clarity—and the sound
of water—a necessary
soothing—and the breeze;

this wooden place where I sit
—water   —wood   and
a cookaburra—   somewhere

behind me   in its metronomic
warbling—   and all around me here
—the bamboo shoots

rise up—the vertical lines
of this wall   the horizontal lines of that
—and here, the third wall weaves—

three bamboo shoots   at a time
in and out   and in—
this sturdy wall of shoots

—a yew tree—*Podocarpus*
Macrophyllus—a stone
bird house and the large

stones set
in these mounds
of tufted grass—here among

the rocks—   I almost interrupt

Across the arced bridge

juniper—   water rolling off a stone

and here, under the shade of this

tree   this long branch that juts out

over the small hills

Southern Magnolias Live Here

Among the pineywoods, not far
from the lake—and there—an egret
on a raft of raw wood—and Fall—

Small turtles lined up—the earth
smells sweet—a naked overcup oak,
Quercus lyrata, a bottomland tree—

graceful in its branches—symmetrical
arcs—bowing down   to earth—
a black crow swoops

and hops—   beneath branches

Sweetgum and Sassafrass

Colorful in Fall—
what an apothecary might
give us to heal
our bodies—

flavor the brown sweet
beverage—of our youth—
and the sweet hard

candy we used to melt
in our young mouths—
and here, the shade

covers my light
and burnable
skin—me—leaning

on a sturdy oak
—a breeze sweeps
slightly through
this wooden space—

across me, the earth—
and across from that,
by the shallow lake—

the tall dry branches
the color of dry grass
raise themselves straight—

upward
reaching
                toward the sky

Man and Woman at The Gardens

"He's missing this whole thing."

She sits there, documenting this terrain—
this lake—the herons—

the egrets—voices of children
across the lake   and him

not even knowing
the missing   not seeing

the houses built
out of hand-hewn oak

red cedar—cypress

The Botanical Gardens: San Antonio, Texas

I want to take you toward the gate
—walk through and up a winding way;

visit what we call The Hill Country
and The Auld House—The Schumachen

House—up to the lake—East Texas
Pineywoods—and maybe, we'll birdwatch

by The Adobe House—"After the first frost,
it really is beautiful," someone says—

talking about the ornamental pear tree,
Pyrus Kawakami—Annie says,

"This tree smells like bread"—and the bees
rollicking—atop the round heads—

Creeping

After months of your disappearing

If I kneel down, about
you, like flowers, the way

they rise, I would crawl up
towards you, not blinking,

my eye open, the other eye
larger, to keep you, I focus—

the way you say *focus,*
the long O—something

about your mouth,
the voice of it, over the lips.

You slipped in, quiet,
the way water seeps

through rocks, & I saw
the slow back of you—

inside me, a pounding,
the way waves break.

Breath, in, a gasp, me—
and the air between me,

and you. A mile. Two.
The leap year. One day

more, to throw off time.
What does time matter?

I am the wildflower,
petals perfumed and velvet,

who wants to rise
against your skin, there,

in the places where we unravel.
I saw you—one moment—

two—who's counting?
I looked down & up again,

& you, a mirage, had slid
out as lightly as you'd come.

I double-took your wave in
the room, the space you inhabit,

though you, like treble
in song, did not see me,

hanging heavy, behind
the shoulder, quiet.

Leaving the Bushes that Bloom

I left before the bushes bloomed,
four years in a place I would call home
despite the small spaces that kept
me still, or not still—   I was there
among the poems and stories—among
the self and others   who tried to take
my self—   I allowed my self
a portion of home, a portion of sky,
and the garden.

I don't even know the name of these
bushes that bear white flowers popping up
each spring; they appear—only three
weeks—out of the year. Always
my favorite time—the day when they'd come
up; and I'd sit outside—   more than awhile,
stare out the window until I could
no longer stand or had to attend

to the world. And today, ironic enough,
they come out, as I pack my last bags
to go to another place I will call home. Oh yes,
I will have the Live Oaks there that stretch
and bend, that almost dance. I will have the trees
that hover and shade—color the space
and grass, the small rolling hills. But I do not
have the bushes that bloom
in spring—   I miss the garden that kept
me for years, that space where I lost
the light, where I sat amidst the blue

plumbagoes—   and, one day, among
earth worms that came up out
of the ground after a long rain.
I sat there, legs and feet extended on a chair
as the thin, long bodies crawled out
and up—   onto   wet cement. I made it back
in, away from them, from the ground
that seemed to swell—

And here, I go, away from this
large garden I grew. From this
large garden where neighbors stopped
to thank me for flowers I'd keep,
put up for the day or the week,
maybe the month—sometimes
even the year, depending
on the sky—the breath in each.

At Christmas, the lights—
in fall, the purple mums
—the rust red leaves.
In summer, salamander pink
stock and the daffodils that popped
up in almost-blinding blooms.

But it was spring that brought me
the white buds that wrapped around
my fence; they'd grown high enough.
I remember, the first year there,
I knew the bushes would fill
—and I waited to see
the foliage each year would bring.
Now, they are florid as fruit.

Late February, I'd start to look
for buds I knew would grow
—this time, too late. On Sunday,
they appeared, and me too busy to look
for long—   I left at the beginning
of that season; but something pulled me
back to that space   led me to come close
for a fraction of an hour   to look again
at the bushes   I always expected
to bloom.

The Way Things Happen

Closing the door on the dark, false light yellows the room and I
await sleep; something stops us, long enough to think; things we wish
we could say—blue dresses in the dark or the light—and the doorways

in and out—of night. Dreams are one way to say I wish I could pray.
Words find a way out—sometimes even mean something—but listen
to this guitar—and the way it might play a body. Not this time.

The escalating scales descend, and those that fall, find a way back—
the wood that plays what so many will not say—and who said music is dead
today? But finding would mean forcing—these notes stay on their own;

the messages are lost; I do not know where I put it down put it down
too fast to remember; too fast. Something about the light and the turn left
and out into the night—grey; near water—clouds; there was music,

and in the dream, dusky; where we think we've lost the light
—but this magical absence of light is blue and grey; I swim in—
almost dreaming it back. The night. It doesn't scare me. I prefer

walking when others sleep. I walk while no one is looking. Quieter,
that way. Just the oaks and the cicadas—a cricket. The sounds
of night. And the dim forgotten light behind a slow-moving cloud;

the moon is white tonight—and here I am, looking at the way.
Who says I am white? I am more red—and this skin, protective shield—
and God is great. The human body. The machine. The way it is made.

And I praise the light; and I praise the day, and the Giver of the day—
and of this sound and of this sound that slows and speeds and rises.
And here it is— that note that note, that place; where I lose the false;

real comes into sight. And the day is what I thank God for because
I cannot stop to pray—I sit here and listen to imaginings; and I love
the people that stay, and I love the people that leave and the days feel

miles away and the days feel miles away and where was Wordsworth
when I was born? Even a name contains the truth—frets up and down
the wooden neck can only take me so far—but far enough, far enough.

I am elevated here, even as I sit in my flesh—the body; even as I sit, I close
the eyes—sound imperative to freeing—remove the day remove the day—
keep it tucked and safe, maybe not too far away. I never liked losing.

Watching the World from a Corner Table

I am the dark shadow
that is unbent—unable
to bend—somehow—
I arrive at this
humility, this re-routing
of space, as it were—

I am the dark
itself—it doesn't matter
what matter is
today—it only feels
to matter—it only feels
to feel this
unbecoming
day—
day in which
I did not become
any thing

What is this color here?
Here, under this beam
of light—it is the shadow
of a shadow—
the wall is here—
by me—I know this—
I touch it
—there is no faith
that needs to explain
this (reality)

Today is dark again,
though the sun is still

here—half-hidden
behind clouds—I
came out in it today—
then lost it
behind the white
and cold grey air

Is air white
or gray?
Is air?

I am always observing things—
I've been told, *You have a wandering eye*

I see the colors of roofs
I see the sign
no one sees—
People rushing by
without looking

Dark Sky

Outside My Coast Boulevard Apartment, La Jolla, California

You are the darkest sky
I've seen. You're black,
you're blue, shades and colors
of green. Come down on me
dark sky, bring yourself low,
cover me like a *mantilla,*
my mother's head cloth.
You are here, dark sky.
Above me. Watching.
Covering. Laying yourself
low above my own darkness.
We are both black, sky.
Sky is your name. You see,
I call you by it. Hush.
There are stars beeping
soundless. I cannot hear them,
but I see them. Watch.
Miniscule headlights waning.
On. Off. They would beep
if I could hear them. Listen. Here
a star. There a star. Stars
all around me. My neck is breaking
I've bent it so far back. I am dizzy
with sky. This is my planetarium,
my private ensconcement, my galaxies
shining, my blue, my dark,
my midnight sky. Hush.

In a San Diego Courtyard

This dark evening, early
December light still
surrounds me

—false light—real light—what is light?

I should be cold here, but I'm not.
Winter bypasses the Pacific.   I sit

by this fountain,
water folding over itself
                 and back;

water has softened the edges it skirts.
Persistence drives a stone mad.

Softening the edges.

They way the world would be
if only we let the water
roll   over the edges

and back.

Accidental Resting

I would never have planned
an hour by a fountain

spiced cider—the air not warm—
not cold

me—the water—rocks
around me—
a slow night

I'm supposed to entertain
the crowd tonight

but for now—I sit, almost
meditating

almost   not guilty

Time

I'll tell you what—we are almost
run over by time—a Faulknerian
thing, perhaps. The ticking
does not stop. Away, away

the hours chime. And us, running
frenzied about, as if we can beat
the clock. But when we stop, somehow,
to rest—or when the head

no longer aches—words—again.
It always happens like this.
They save themselves up
during the busy days—

When we make ourselves sit
by the waters of a river,
by the floating
water sliding down—

When we sit awhile
in this constant place
of beginning—the night entering
its expected hour—

It is then—here—that the words
make their way out. Here
they unfold. When the mind is quiet,
and the river is not.

II.

Wildflower. Stone.

out
To the yellow flowers
Quivering in sluggish heat...

The tall flowers in my dreams are
Big as the First State Bank ...

They have women's names,
With mouths like where
Babies come from ...

These yellow flowers
Go on forever.
Almost to Detroit.
Almost to the sea ...

—Yusef Komunyakaa

Wildflower. Stone.

El Paso del norte, something holy
about that. The Pass of the North.

A place of passage, a place of entry,
a tunnel through where we began,
begin, continue to begin. Every day—

a white new sun unfolding,
sun so bright, we cannot focus;
sometimes we are blinded

by this wild, wild light. No other sun
like this . . .

I.

I was born   under
El Paso's desert sky,

The Pass of the North
there—   between

the Franklins, The Organ Mountains;
there—   with Ciudad Juarez,

Mexico—at my side;
with Southern New Mexico

near me   I was born
where three cultures sang,

met   began their turning.

The arid places
southwest of our state—

a constancy,
an open slate—

~ ~ ~

I remember living
near Scenic Drive;
Father and Mother and I

would ride up the long,
slow-curving hill
from our street—

at the foot   of the mountain
        —tires slowly crawling
and curving   up the hot

        asphalt—along the rim
of the road;   and our city
named that landing

Rim   Road   —there
among the sun, the cactus
and rock—there, looking out

on our city   and our
sombrero-shaped   Civic Center
—the buildings   down in that

cavernous space   between
mountains—the color of sand—
were important when I   was

five   and six; I remember
             my father naming
them   in his daily list

of things   to do: El Paso National
Bank. State National. Southern Union
Gas.   El Paso Electric.   Part

of our place.

~ ~ ~

And so, whenever we'd drive up that road
named *Brown,* up along the rim—I'd look

to my left—at the dry mountains—try to name
—the banks, the buildings—the streets—

that curved like snakes   through our wide
spaces—I'd look down   —and see

the tall or wide buildings, their glass shining
like crystal   in our white sun. And there

it stood   our Roman-like high school,
proclaiming the name   of our town—El Paso

High: proud   and regal   and strong
there—in the middle of our city, like a coliseum—
with its grand pillars   and many stairs.

~ ~ ~

And when we arrived
at the top of Rim Road,
we would always look out.

In day, it looked wide
and open—somehow endless

and safe; at twilight, it began

its turning. Its miraculous colors
swooned out of sky—

fire, fire—everywhere;
red and orange

bronze

molten
fiery
liquid
sky

I would look out of windows
to see
this happening—

Great sky down.

Sun spread like fire
across our vast place;

and the closer we came
to night—dusk took on
its regal blues—

fuchsia, purple
periwinkle   and
the deeper   violets
                  amethyst

This is how
the miracle would take
its final shape

for the night—

We'd look out over the rim
in our descent

back down
to our home, or up

again, we'd look below us
at the shimmering
phosphorescent lights

electrifying
our night—

~ ~ ~

City of lights.
City of lights.

There, in that large, circular space
between earth and sky.

~ ~ ~

Scenic Drive.

We would always take
visitors along

that way, silhouettes
of cacti, yucca, and rock

skirting the road that wound
like a holy trail   down

through our night.

~ ~ ~

And sometimes, we'd drive to Las Cruces,
there in southern   New Mexico.

I love the name.

The crosses.

Something holy
about that.

Old Mesilla: history, churches
and stone; the long drive out

to our neighboring city
and state   would take us by and through
some farmland—

cotton fields, perhaps—
through our El Paso
upper valley, the long green fields—

and if
we drove up the interstate,
we'd see

this expansive sky

sun beaming through glass
our windows   reflecting

the light—

~ ~ ~

A long open space
from here to there—

How close can two bodies be?

~ ~ ~

And we'd drive into   the New Mexican terrain,

And we'd travel up   flat roads

where large wooden carts   stood, filled
with watermelon, cantaloupe   and truckloads

of long green chili. I could smell their sharp, sweet scent
in our air. We would bend, sometimes, to pick

some out   of burlap bags stacked
side-by-side   fill   our own bags up

take the green fruit   in loose bundles—home—
roast them,
peel the skins   slowly   down,
keeping

the fleshy fruit in tact—
fill each with cheese—beef—
whatever we would find.

And once we slid   our trays
of stuffed   or unstuffed chili

into our stoves   our houses
would give off   a wild scent

specific to our place

          our land
          our missions

          our space

~ ~ ~

We neighbored close to that small town—

Las Cruces

The Crosses . . .

Old Mesilla—

our neighboring spot,
the square that held a church and shops

and cafes; furniture chiseled
out of wood, candles burning their scent

through dry air, a gazebo
in the middle of a small central park.

The Double Eagle

where so many of us
would take our lunch,
our coffee,
our tea—
a small theater that sat
only two or three
at tables

while we watched
films—ate sugared sweets

—drank dark
or light
wine.

~ ~ ~

It didn't feel far from home. Our deserts bound us
in their making— land and earth and sky

—the periphery of our place.   We entered each others' cities
like the houses   of siblings.   We always knew

we were welcome   part   of each others' space.

~ ~ ~

And maybe   we would drive   through Santa Teresa,
the long dirt roads   that took us out   and up   into

a secret.   Mountain Vista   Road   its name tells
of what we see.   I stood and sat on a porch once

at *Casa de Suenos*   House of Dreams   twice or more
—there, looking out   at a dark, dark night—and across from me

—straight across   I saw   the long, winding trail
I knew so well   lit up   with white moving lights. Transmountain

Drive—far, far away   lit up and dreaming   but close enough   to see
car lights peeking   and shimmering down

the curved road.   They snaked down   at a regular   and endless
and silent   pace   lighting up the road between   darkness—

darkness—on either side; trail of steady headlights in their downward curving
glide, inching towards me like   a silent river   soundless and flowing

through black night—   And above me—   the stars
The Big Dipper   the great constellations   clear,   in this desert

sky—   city lights   so far, away   and the river
that runs   through our land   and that river that   divides

Mexico   from our United States   and the river
that is so familiar   to our place: *Santa Teresa, Juarez, El Paso;*

this same river   that divides   two countries, somehow
connects us—   *water—water*   *everywhere*

a river   we somehow call   ours.

~ ~ ~

And the long drive back at night;
if we were lucky—we'd catch the setting
of our shared sun. The liquid falling-down

of sky—down to greet us, to paint
us in its multicolored shades and sheets.

~ ~ ~

And if we had time, we'd veer left,
on our way from our neighboring New Mexican state,
back to our West Texas place—

and if we had time, and if . . .
we would veer up and into   the majestic mountains
—our westernmost sliver of state,

there—   up   and up   and up
We couldn't climb high enough   in our cars, curving
towards the light   where we would park and look out

and down—crows swooping in   and out
of this cavernous space—mountains at our back,
mountains to our right   to our left—

right in front   of us.   These great mountains
proclaimed   our night was here. Or coming.

~ ~ ~

Whether the sky was orange and fiery
in its setting light   whether it was purple or blue
or sapphire   in the coming on of night

whether it was black and lit electric
with stars   and stars   and stars
it was *our* magical place—

Transmountain Drive

Trans Mountain Road

We called it so many
different things, but we knew MOUNTAIN

was at the core—of the slightly different names.
We knew our mountains   were holy—and high

and happening. Regal rocks that stood
against a slant   of a mountain wall,

occasional brush   crawling in
and under   rocks—

~ ~ ~

And when the wildflowers would bloom,
we'd look down into a sea

of canary yellow
sun yellow
fire   yellow

liquid
and bright

and glorious.

~ ~ ~

Wildflower. Stone.

Wildflower. Stone.

These

are what we claim.

Mountain.

Sky.

Sun. Moon. Night.

Stars that shimmer
in phosphorescent light.

~ ~ ~

Even under our sun that heats and breaks and cracks the earth and sand,
and even in our rough and sometimes much too dry land,

we are florid   and fecund.

~ ~ ~

Come night sky, break—

cast your many-colored light
on our roofs,

on the tops of houses,
on our wild, wild
windy nights;

sometimes dust mists our air,

sometimes
it does

and what is not beautiful
about that?

~ ~ ~

Sometimes I feel

small granules of sand

on my face,

and are we not made of earth?

It reminds me of how

sand and water
make a body.

Water.

River.

Earth.

We are dust and water
molded into   flesh

and this is the ground
of our making.

II.

And when I drive from my Hill Country place,
and when I drive through the green, green hills

and foliage of Boerne   Kerrville   Comfort,
the central Texas space of *water, water*

everywhere—floods and fields and green
and rock, and through cowboy prairie   Sonora,

Ozona, the long dry place   occasional brush
and shrub   scattered   between rock.

A wildflower   a stone,   sometimes appear
side-by-side   or a field of flowers rushing by—

outside my window, unexpected
—in a dry field;   and when the sun begins

its late afternoon yellowing   after veering into
Marathon, somewhere over *The Gage*   or back on I-10

driving   by Fort Stockton,   then I know
I am halfway home   to the history of that place.

and I see the sun's setting   in Van Horn,
smoke-purple mountains in my rearview

mirror, sometimes their peaks covered at the tip
with snow;   dry, cold wind   against my face;

air blows through an open window—   and then the names
I know, coming back: Marfa, the lights,

Sierra Blanca—the grand snow-capped mountains.
Allamore Hot Wells   Texas Mountain Trail,

and there it is, intact   EL PASO COUNTY LINE

and then   the familiar names: Tornillo, 1 mile,
next 7 exits.   Fabens, 1.   El Paso, 28.

Clint.   San Elizario, 1.   And the lights begin
their spreading out—

III.

And then, there is the drive
from San Antonio   toward
                  the Texas coast.

Farther away from desert,

the coming towards
bountiful

beautiful   water.

Two edges of the world.

Two edges of the world.

Desert.

Water.

Possible
to have

two lovers.

Water calls me,
and I'm feeling
Mexico

again—

coming up on it.

Coming into it
—a third skin.

Something in me
leaps   at the thought
of nearing home.

What is a country?

I keep finding myself
welcome
and coming
into

different parts

of the world.

Entering
The Rio Grande
Valley.

Poppy-yellow flowers
flying by
                and past me—

looking into
my rearview,

I drive headlong
towards

the coast.

I am starving for water.

I rejoice in sky
in sun
in sound.

Field of yellow flowers,
bright as sun,
under a blue-white sky.

The clouds are lower here,
coming closer,
to water.

~ ~ ~

Palm trees in wind announce this terrain,
and the clouds *are* lower here,
and I *am* near water.

We are mostly water—and so—
when water finds us—
or we—find it—
there is   no other   healing.

~ ~ ~

I have traveled through desert,
the Kerrville hills,
cowboy prairie   and now—

this coastal sky—

I revel in the roads and fields
of this fine and seemingly endless
state—Rockport in rain—

Corpus Christi   body
                              of Christ.

~ ~ ~

I am hungry and stop by *Snoopy's* by the water.
This cigarette smells good here, in this coastal setting.

And the gulls   and the two o'clock sun
on these waters.   I sit first, directly under sun,

savor the burning   of the light. And when that becomes too much,
and when that becomes   I move inside,

sit in a dark, wooden-floored room, still
looking out on water, but the fan here breathes a cooler kind of air

on this damp skin. Somehow, sitting in
is not a satisfying place for me to be.   I walk back out into

a middle space   not the unshaded place
of the afternoon's hard beginning   not in the cool inside air,

but outside   on a deck   watching
the light. The gulls. The boats. And here—a tall and graceful bird tightropes

its way across the fat wooden beam of fence. The sun
is almost touchable here—over water. There is a sea-breeze

that flows cool   under this awning at which I have found
a place to write.   I don't want   to leave.

~ ~ ~

But then I go,
back to North Padre's bay,
Fortuna Bay,
where I will sleep
for two nights.

Purple martins,
blue herons,
white egrets, and
the oleanders,
white

or powder pink,

bougainvillea,
even   a banana tree.

John and Jackie on the boat.
The clouded purple sunset.

The pink swept sky.

~ ~ ~

After the boat ride, I climb
a few steps onto my balcony—

look out over the bay
an hour before night.

There are families
in these houses

across Fortuna Bay.
I sit here, on a lamp-lit

upper deck
—reading

above water.
Words. Water.

The florid nature
of them—

~ ~ ~

And I look across
the shimmering surface

of what seems a lake—
onto   back porches,

allowed to peek   through glass
houses.   And so I seek

the silences of night.
Me   above water.

~ ~ ~

The breeze is one degree
from what I would call cool,

but the air is balmy as salve,
and the water laps

at the edges of a boat;
and the breeze sways this flag

more than gently in this night,
and the stars dot this sky,

somehow spread,
as sky would have them.

~ ~ ~

A mosquito tries its damndest
to taste my skin, creature

of this nearly dank,
yet breezy night;

and I revel in this silence,
in this shut mouth,

in no one taking my attention
away from water—

the boats—the shimmering surface
of the water's light.

~ ~ ~

And after the water becomes as black as it will get,
I move down to the pool and the large wooden deck,

lie on a lounging chair, looking out on what seems a sea.
Almost meditating.   I stare at midnight blue bay,

the ripples it makes   under moonlight.

~ ~ ~

Next morning, I leave the bay.
Next step of the day,

I go to the seawall—
walk by the beach;

though it is not as blue
as I would like water to be—

it is still water, and that
is where   I believe

we were born.

~ ~ ~

Mid-afternoon and I'm back at the bay,
stretched out on a lounge chair and gazing

at ripples, two feet away. I stare hard at them,
and I begin   my floating.   The deck

has become a barge,
and I am floating   —far—far away—

buoyed up and bobbing,
transcendental   meditation.

I understand now.

~ ~ ~

Then evening in downtown Corpus:
Shoreline. Water Street. These are the names

that call me in. A desire for water—
and across the shore, the lights: green, red,

gold—and the lit towers. The breeze—
blue nocturnal pulse—lights on a large boat.

~ ~ ~

Next day Port Aransas,
The Dennis Dreyer Municipal Harbor,

I see a woman flicking scales
off a fish—the fish, in her left hand.

I hear the sounds first, a hard
type of shaving—like playing
a washboard, the knife poised

and firm in her right.

She plays that scaly skin
up and down. The sound

of learning.

~ ~ ~

She dips the fish
she holds tight
in her left hand

into   a white bucket
of water—slightly red—

darker than pink—
          swirls it around

in the liquid;   sits—there—
on the almost-square

rectangular rocks
that jag   up

or down   in rows
on this slight incline—

long legs spread out
as she works—

huddled around the bucket
where she dips the fish's body

into   the bloody water,
her head bent slightly

down   over it;
her and her visor,

pink shirt,
khaki shorts,

and the color—
of blood.

~ ~ ~

She is there, at work,
in this hot Port Aransas sun.

Fishermen.

The piers
are full of them.

~ ~ ~

And there, the large boats
are gliding down;   and over here,

the tri-floor houses stacked
almost against   each other,

colorful in this light—
one is peach;   one, darker

than coral; another—mint green.
These   are the colors

of summer.

~ ~ ~

I ask a woman how to get to Rockport from here. She says I have to board a ferry. Me and my car. I am first in line, here in the middle lane, and I see the *B.L. Deberry* pulling up at the dock—Ramp 4—I have never done this before. All these cars aboard, lined up in rows, poised and ready to drive off after landing. Taillights looking out at water. I can see the faces. And the state police overlook our driving out.

~ ~ ~

4:40. Driving into Rockport.
A little cooler here. More overcast.

Water, water
—everywhere,

and the palms swaying—leaning
in wind   endless circles of water.

Breezy. More movement in these bodies.

Key Allegro.
Fulton Beach.

It's beautiful here.

No wonder everyone   is smiling.

~ ~ ~

And I sit on the long peripheral back deck
at *The Lighthouse Inn,* a few feet from buoyancy.

These waters are active.   Rolling.   Forward stroking,
millions of invisible swimmers   lapping the sea.

I see them now, invisible as they are—
one arm forward; the other arm arcs,

or a breaststroke. Bobbing. And the water hits
the low wall, graceful   in its breaking.

And the wind here is high, and fresh,
and blowing.   This place is so large.

And the seagulls flying by.

~ ~ ~

Then the sad driving out.
These waters seem endless,
driving along the side of the sea.

Seagrass swaying in wind

and trees across from water
sway in grace   from the movement

water and wind   have cast on them.

I'm not happy
about leaving.

~ ~ ~

I come back into Corpus again, large body

of water; I see the North Padre sign,
                                        coming back
through—on my way
                                        to San Antonio—

hard for me   not to veer left, onto
SPID—
        something about this stretch

of places makes me want   to stay.

So many different skies, depending
on the geography
                of the place.

And a few miles out of Corpus,
                    these

planted rows, diagonal in their placement,

speed by—

        They remind me   of the valleys

in and around   El Paso, the tall fields;

but these have a movement   all their own

    under their   cool   sky—

~ ~ ~

I am 100 miles away from home

and the sun bright and coming
down—next to Lake Corpus,

2 miles from Mathis,
and still a ways to go.

I'll be driving   in the dark
again—I can never lean out of day

in time—I don't want to leave
these geographies   in their dancing.

~ ~ ~

From the coast to here, riffs

of sky and cloud   and seagrasses

swaying   in sea breeze—

then, before home, blue-green

fields—and the sky is still

coastal in the shedding

or unshedding   of its light.

And before I know it, I am miles away

from Pleasanton. To my right,

off Highway 35, somewhere

before 99—and Whitsett, I see a tall man,

pressed jeans and creased. Black t-shirt,

and the straw hat;   in one fell swoop,

he swings   open   a gate,

and I cannot stop   the looking.

~ ~ ~

Clouds to my left
slide by an orange sun
masking
the light.

Behind me, now far away—

Rockport,
Port Aransas,
Fortuna Bay

—North Padre and its blue
plumbagos,
            Corpus Christi's shoreline
at night—   so much water.

~ ~ ~

And this coming back to land—
is solid.

        Earth beneath me
and around.

        San Antonio 57.

And the bridges over rivers.

Atascosa River—

Atascosa County.

A beautiful name—

sitting silent in its sibilance.

~ ~ ~

I never like turning
the headlights on. I keep

trying—flicking them
into play—I turn them off

again—try once more—
Not dark enough, yet.

I savor the last quiet shades
of day; interstates stitching

one county to the next.

IV.

And so I try to find my place
between desert and water.

I was born in the arid flat land
at the foot of the dry mountains,

and the river there   creates borders
between countries. We are connected

to Mexico   because of that
river—   *Rio Bravo—Brave River.*

Rio Grande—Big River;   it claims
Mexico begins   where we end

at the other shoulder   of water,
a skip of a rock away—   and it is a thin body

of water that runs   through our town.
Our desert, strong, under—an unending open sky,

the mystery of silences;   stars
are brighter   out here—

comfort of home—snakes that crawl
in-between large crevices of rock,

crickets   and their chirping—   sounds
of desert   dust kicking up

behind the wheels   of a car
road stretching   up   or down

between dry mountains.
Arid land expansive geography

and the night mountains encircling
—cradling this city's lights.

We are the other side of water.

~ ~ ~

And then the seas, the water itself, lapping
against the boats—sheets of water glisten

under a sharp sun. Just looking at sky, I can tell
whether I am in the desert or far away

—from that place— something happens close
to the coast and into it. I look up

at this seaward sky— feel water
reflecting somehow off of it. I know—

depending on the clouds or the occasional
repression of light— I know by looking up

I am coming closer
to water.

~ ~ ~

Even in the desert, there is water,
a river that runs in the middle of a city,
dry and brown as it may be,

all the way up
from Colorado, funnels
down into
El Paso's terrain—

and I think of Elroy Bode's
childhood river
in the Texas Hill Country,

and I make that river
somehow mine,

translate it into
my El Paso place,

my *Rio Grande,*
    Big River,

and I recall,
from whatever sky I am under
at the time—

I recall

> *I walked near the river that went beside our town... I was there in that place... I was alone in the two o'clock silence of our world... It wore a groove in me as deep as memory... it was the heart of my childhood.*

~ ~ ~

This is where
I learned
the importance of water,
there
in a dry place.

Where I began to ask
the questions of race,
and countries,
and borders

where I realized
mountains
do not have to be green.

~ ~ ~

There is
a paradisiacal place
where mountains are purple
at dawn—   at night,

and brown
at day.

I never knew
how beautiful

our dry and mountainous space
was to me,

until I left

and dreamt nightly

of sunset over
the Franklins,

of crows swooping in
and out

of our cavernous space.

And it is in dreams
that these mountains
come back   to me

in the absence of that light

of the great and endless sky
that I have lost
for a day

or a night.

            Then, I see water,

almost drowning in it—

driving over bridges
            in Corpus—

Water to my left.

        Water to my right.

Water bleeding somehow
        into sky's edge

                        into space

water stretched out
as far as heaven,

as far as our eye   can see.

    I can tell the earth
is a circle   from here.

III.

Yellow Buds of the Desert; Birds of Paradise

And the earth being of that celestial ancestry, remembers this season before its creatures do... if you mark their places day by day you will see that stones weighing many tons have begun to move across level fields, carving deep grooves in the out-croppings, and you may be able to hear their voices—muffled rumblings... so that you remember tales of caverns full of beards at the end of which spirits without age slept with their crowns on the tables.

—**W. S. Merwin**

Mountain Vista

There is a crucial relationship between
a person and a place, I believe. This is
a sacred equation.
— N. Scott Momaday

Mountain Vista,
an appropriate name,
turning left onto
your street of dreams
at night—at daybreak,
in high sun,
whatever the time—

There are your mountains,
Oh Great Sky, lining the rim
of this night,

and beneath them, there,
quiet, trembling, at the foot
of your great and purple
magnificent hills—
The Pass of the North

City I knew,
City I will always know,
the lights shimmering

in the upstroke and down-
stroke of our desert
heat—between heat

and breeze and sky
and dirt—between heaven
and this solid earth

There you lie—
sure as remembrance—
I have always seen you
here—standing solid
        behind my back—

Upon Driving

Santa Teresa, New Mexico (five miles from El Paso)

A right on Koogle Road—
driving a horseback-like beat,
bobbing up and down roads,
ripples of small rock and earth
crunching beneath tires.

Almost 2 a.m.—and this quiet
night—car windows down.
The crickets chirp a living hum
of sorts—in their tenor throats,
singing me in on the dark
starlit roads. The stars are out here

tonight. No city lights
to blur them out. Out here,
it is God and sky—uncontaminated
land—cool breeze against
this clammy skin. Hard not to be
alive. Not to revel in the living
breath—every second we are given,
a gift. And here I am—driving—in this
magical absence of light.

Quiet.
Quiet.   Essential
to be quiet—in order
that we hear the soothing
voice   of God

Star light
Star bright
I wish I may
I wish I might
Keep breathing

in order that I may see
the light.

This Beautiful Morning

I watched the sun
rise today from
my father's house—
pink-in-its-disguise

and the white light,
now yellow, bright
on this dry mountain
at my shoulder—

Here, two trees
marry—leaves inter-
mingle—branches
soft upon the other;

they seem similar
though this one
here, before me,
I can touch it

with my raised
hand, sitting—
a softer shade
a softer bundle

of needles clustered
on each branch—
This tree
is the woman—

above it, similar,
yet not—the green
a millishade
more yellow—

the coarser cluster
unable to sway
in air like that.
It is grace that names

the female—
and my father's
garden—'round
about me.

My father's garden

is full of weeds now—
I am okay with that—as a matter of fact
I am stunned by their grace—their appearance since
May—I came to say *Sabah il khayr*

to kiss the forehead of a father
one late Sunday morning—and they
took me
by surprise—me gasping
deep—almost smiling   standing there,
by the bay
window, bringing in
the light

There they were—
what we call weeds—
florid and high
—and the richest green—
little yellow buds
peeking their heads   between what seemed
fields of gathering
fern—I was amazed
at the fecundity of forms

of grass
of bright yellow

happenings. Our field
was near-covered
with them.

Father walked in to see
what all my great commotion
was about—he smiled, shyly,
almost ashamed   and said,

Badnah nik'lah-on—
"We are going to pull them out."

The man he was would never have
allowed such rampant things—
But I said, "No, Baba. These
are beautiful." He looked and tried to see,
and I think he agreed
after the looking.

Two feet high, maybe three
of feathery green—what seemed a field
of small wild flowers
at the tips of stems   bright—
the color of sun

—just enough space
between them
for wind   to play
and breezes
to sway stems   perhaps

his field had been
so dry for so long

they remind me
of his kept garden
that curled around our house.

The grass was always there
and watered—as if we
expected it to be—
us running
through our busy days—

I assume we never thought
of how it stayed—Father
watering, placing the hose,
curled like a garden snake
among grass—perhaps
that is why our lawn
was never as evenly colored
as the neighbors' yards—

he would shift—after so long,
the placement of the coiled hose
to dryer spots   rotate
every so often, the fielding
of water—

and so,
there were yellow
spots and tufts of grass

that water
did not reach. But there was always

grass   and the bricks and stones
he'd use to build low circles around the trees
—we saw them bud and grow

yield his proud fruit—always asking the guests
if they'd like to see
the garden,
explaining proudly—
pointing each one out   and the naming began:

apricot, fig, plum

mish-mosh, tteen, khokhh

—and the grapevines that crawled
along the stone
fence—   so high, grape leaves covered
the wall—   and the grapes, hanging heavy
in their descending bodies
along the periphery
of our place—

and then
the *daly*—the place he built
out of chicken-wire and wood—
holding the vines up

training them
to grow
this way   or that
—what others might call
a coop   we'd enter this large
sub-garden through a fence that unlatched—
chicken-wire high above us
and all around
to keep

the birds out—to protect
the grapes—not pecked at yet

Father would slowly walk
amid the *daly,* raise his arms high up
to pick the pickable ones—

And I'd follow him
—put them in
a deep, long tray
until it was full—

arms heavy with fruit
        and overflowing

Picking grapes—
                                        in my father's proud yard.

Only the Sky Can Heal the Frightened Eye

Mother is not well.
Just a happening to trip
        the brain's wire into a place
        that repeats
        that shouts
        that brings out the wild eye.
To see this slow happening.

What brought us to this?

She called my name to see
A star!

She pulled the slow curtain to the right,
Looked out into the surrounding night,
Smiling and bright-eyed,
She pointed out the star in the dark desert sky
With an innocent, open, glorious eye.

Upon Leaving The House of Dreams

The wild sadness
in leaving this sky—
the sun   the stars

set against
pitch black—
the desert night
—dust kicking up
as I drive

—dust, air, sky, night
stars that shimmer
in phosphorescent light—

windows open—
I ride looking out
and up
    at this
    great sky—

    and the stars

    they seem closer
    tonight
    than far

and the breeze
blowing through

    this corridor—

ocotillo, purple sage,
oleander, pink
and white

these yellow buds
of the desert
birds of paradise

the yucca plants' stalks
raised up in the light

A Psalm for a Mother

Mother Mary, first mother, first light,
light in darkness, come to us. Our own mothers—
far away. Past light. Who is counting
the stars? A child, perhaps, will
remember the odd night where Mother's voice
rang out as if afraid, or wounded. A call for us
to come. And I came, Mother, you standing
at the window—wonderment of a child then,
you there, surprised by light. Looking up
at a star you pointed out. Calling me
to see— Wonderment and worship,
the star woke you into light, after a night of fear,
after a night filled with the lost
look in your eye. Mother, the only things I know
that heal, include light, light from light, and stars
and the Maker of them. I pray with you here
under a lit sky, I know you are there, Mother,
listening—among stars.

After Mama

Near Balmoreah

The flat-topped hills
are not like you, Mother,

you are arched
—like the dome

of a rainbow—
where light colors

the sky—and leaves
us looking upward

and dreaming—
coming into

Ozona—and the light
here is beautiful

—and you are light,
Mother—you are light

and now, you span
the sky—and this mountain

is a steeple, and you are
praying there   and you

are everywhere

Statue of the Sleeping

Our time here is short. We return to myth
for life. Ariadne and her thread lead us somehow
through the maze of what we call a life. One myth
goes beyond what we know, how we know it,
extends the days. Something to believe in.
Even if—a dream—

Before we know it, a sarcophagus might hold
a body, a beloved—even ours; and before we blink
—the maze leads us here, inside a box. We soften
the moment—a box within which we place
a body, sure not to shift—soften the passing
with the shape

of a woman reclining above the still
body within a box. Our bodies, their own box
—before we find them one to keep in. Therefore,
we are, when breathless and still, a box within
a box—make it ivory or stone, line it with
dolphins who leap

out of water; the trajectory of an arc. We
will dance out of this, we will arc along
with these dancers leaping in water—in
the afterlife—in our own life—or myth.
Female or male. Myth or man
or mother of man.

No matter the geography of our dancing,
or the time of this dance here, or there,

wherever there is—no matter the timelessness
of it, or the limited time it taunts us with,
no matter if we dance in what was then
Tyre, near ancestral waters,

maternal earth and river; no matter if we dance back
in—or on the Roman earth, whether in or out—
of a Grecian urn, we will arc—above this
season of dry bones, arc above buoyant water
in our leaping, between water and sky, between between.
Memory is larger—and stronger—than stone.

Listening to "Main Street"

Leaving Ozona

What can I say? Who shall describe
the light? It is like an epidemic; it is
like your love.
—William Carlos Williams

I did not know
I loved this place
so much—   maybe

it's the light
in its downward glide—
maybe the flat-topped hills—

this yellow sunlit sky—
maybe

Bob Seger curving
down the road with me—

the geometry of space—

the day is almost colorless
in this evanescent light.

Something of heaven here.

Sloping walls
of limestone

and the road curves
and rises
toward the light—

between two high walls
of white rock

I funnel
through.

And here—
the sun hits high
across this sloping

white wall—

and I never knew
you were
so beautiful—

though I've been here
more than once—

more than that—

and never
like this—
have you looked
this golden—

    cat-tails swaying

    in the light.

Driving through Ozona

They have cut through
this mountain
of limestone rock

21 miles from Ozona
heading East—
made a way for us

—semis smoking—
pipesmoke
charring chrome—

18 wheels roll alongside—
I step on the gas—
pass a Ballard sign

on the slate blue cab
of a semi-truck;
6 o'clock

and the streets are hot—
pavement thick
with heat

Driving 90 now—
I roll the windows down,
as long as I can—

this
unbearable heat
is somehow sweet

—though I must raise
the windows up
until this heat

has passed—chilled
a degree—or ten—
or two—the sun

will come down soon,
and I'll be here—
on this 2-lane road

they call a highway—
I should hit Sonora
before dusk

head on in
through that clear blue light
I expect

Driving from El Paso to San Antonio

There's a sad part
of the afternoon.

I love the first
light—and the whiteness
of the desert then.

And I love
the high noon
hour—and the sun
that beams.

Intensity
and becoming.
Even the few
hours after that
are livable.

Me in the stream
of the given day,
somewhere in-between
between.

But then
it comes—
the hour
after that—
before the darkness—
the end of day—
the end of light—

It says something
about
the sadness
of endings.
Things that leave us,
the lost beginning.

And when that yellow
hue has trailed
its final sad note—
there is still
light—

a post-light
not yet sunset—
light outside
light—sadness
past—the lost day
past—and me
in the middle
of that short hour.

And now
in my rearview,
a strong white sheath
spreads itself out
across this sky
—white again—
no sadness here.

I ride alongside
a semi—
following the same
blue sky
that leads us
shortly
into night.

This cool
evening—
and the windmills
blow—just past
Monahans.

The sun
behind me—
easting its orange,
its lavender light.

And I await
the evening
sky—

coming closer
to home.

San Antonio Winter

Only a moment—not more—
of pink—darker than pink—
Somewhere between pink
and light—sweeping
this January sky—
It is more like Spring
than Winter here—
in this city
of a Saint—

2009-2010 Books from Pecan Grove Press:

Ahl, Liz. *Luck.* 2010.
ISBN: 978-1-931247-75-7 $7

Aitches, Marian. *Ours Is a Flower.* 2010.
ISBN: 978-1-931247-78-8 $15

Balcárcel, Rebecca. *Palabras in Each Fist.* 2010.
ISBN: 978-931247-60-6 $15

Carbó, Nick. *Chinese, Japanese, What Are These?* 2009.
ISBNJ: 978-1-931247-64-1 $15

Case, Susana H. *The Cost of Heat.* 2009.
ISBN: 978-1-931247-81-8 $7

Frost, Helen. *as if a dry wind.* 2009.
ISBN: 978-1-931247-66-5 $15

Greene, Jeffrey. *Beautiful Monsters.* 2010.
ISBN: 978-1-931247-77-1 $15

Harper, Cynthia A. *Lipstick.* 2009.
ISBN: 1-931247-73-3 $15

Kemp, Robin. *This Pagan Heaven.* 2009.
ISBN: 978.1.931247-64-1 $8

LaVilla-Havelin, Jim. *Counting.* 2010.
ISBN: 978-1-931247-80-1 $15

Levin, Carol. *Red Rooms and Others.* 2009.
ISBN: 978-1-931247-57-3 $8

Moore, Trey. *Some Will Play the Cello.* 2010.
ISBN: 978-1-931247-70-2. $17

Pettit, Holly. *To One Who Lives on the Mainland.* 2010.
ISBN: 978-1-931247-71-9 $17

Reeves, Phoebe. *The Lobes and Petal of the Inanimate. 2009.*
ISBN: 978-1-931247-65-8 $8

Rojas Joo, Juan Armando. *Rió Vertebral / Vertebral River.*
2009. ISBN: 978-1-931247-60-3 $18

Saidi, Mo H. *The Color of Faith. 2010.*
ISBN: 978-1-931247-79-5. $15.

Witte, Francine. *First Rain.* 2009.
ISBN: 978-1-931247-61-0 $8

For a complete listing of Pecan Grove Press titles,
please visit our website at
http://library.stmarytx.edu/pgpress